Multi-Format Layout Workbook

Imperial Rectangular Grid

Journal Delight

2018

How to use this book

Thank you for choosing the *Multi-Format Layout Workbook*. Fulfil your potential whenever you set up pages, design leaflets or create books or journals. The workbook provides:

- 160 pages to doodle, sketch, draw or write,
- a ¼" rectangular bullet grid on each page,
- markings for 12 common paper sizes.

The following paper sizes are marked on each page:

Common name	Imperial (")	Metric (mm)	Most popular in	Nr
Letter	$11 \times 8\frac{1}{2}$	279 × 216	US	-
B5	9.8 × 6.9	250 × 176	Europe and others	1
Octavo	9 × 6	229 × 152	US	2
Kiku 5	8.9 × 5.9	227 × 151	Japan	3
Half letter	$8\frac{1}{2} \times 5\frac{1}{2}$	216 × 140	US	4
A5	8.3 × 5.8	210 × 148	Europe and others	5
Junior Legal	8 × 5	203 × 127	US	6
Shirokuban 6	7.4 × 5	188 × 127	Japan	7
B6	6.9 × 4.9	176 × 125	Europe and others	8
A6	5.8 × 4.1	148 × 105	Europe and others	9
B7	4.9 × 3.5	125 × 88	Europe and others	10
A7	4.1 × 2.9	105 × 74	Europe and others	11

Use the full page to work with the *Letter* format. All the other paper sizes start from the larger corner at the bottom close to the spine. To set up your page, just look out for the smaller corners (⌐ or ¬) showing the correct number. If you would like to create a layout in the popular *Octavo* format for example, hold the larger edge at the bottom close to the spine and look out for the little edge showing the number 2. These two edges define the papersize. To work on the smaller European *B6* format, simply hold the larger edge at the bottom close to the spine and look out for the little edge showing the number 8.

A word of caution: the purpose of this book is to support layout and design – not high-precision engineering. Therefore, paper markings can be off by 1mm or by ¹/₃₂". Just to let you know...

$\sqrt{1}$
$\sqrt{2}$
$\sqrt{3}$
$\sqrt{4}$
$\sqrt{5}$
$\sqrt{6}$
$\sqrt{7}$
$\sqrt{8}$
$\sqrt{9}$
$\sqrt{10}$
$\sqrt{11}$